I'm Molly

I'm Molly

All rights reserved
Copyright 2018 Major Mitchell.

All characters and events portrayed in
this book are real.

Reproduction in any manner,
in whole are part, in English or any
other languages, or otherwise without the written
permission of publisher is prohibited.

For information contact: Shalako Press
P.O. Box 371, Oakdale, CA 95361-0371
http://www.shalakopress.com

ISBN: 978-0-9990070-7-5

Photographs provided by Major and Judy Mitchell
Cover layout and design by Karen Borrelli
Editor: Judy Mitchell

PRINTED IN THE UNITED STATES OF AMERICA

I'm Molly.
What is your name?

My mommy took pictures when I was a baby.

I love my mommy and daddy.

They feed me yummy dog food to eat. What do you like to eat?

Daddy gives me baths.
Do you like baths?

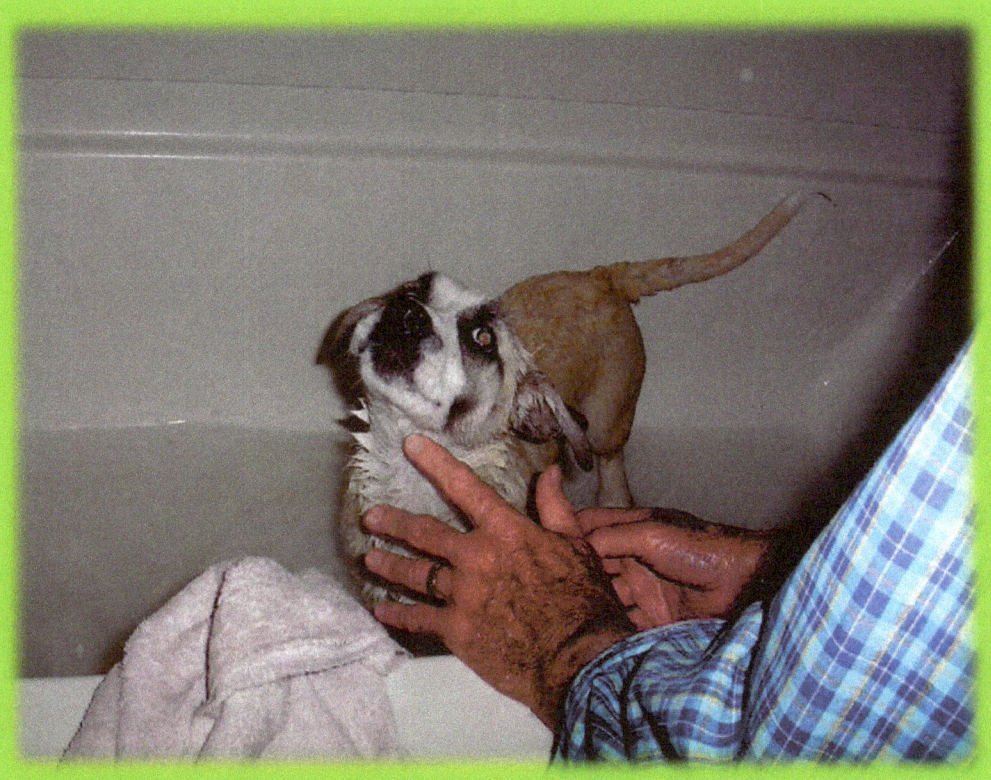

I like to play "Catch Me If You Can" with my daddy. I always win.

These are my favorite toys. I have a gorilla and an elephant. What do you see?

This is my friend Baby. She's very nice and runs fast too.

This is my friend Andy and his family. Andy is a lizard and has a blue tummy. What color is your tummy?

Here are some of my favorite treats. What treats do you like to eat?

I roll over for a treat.

See how fast I run?
Can you catch me?

I like to take long walks with my daddy and see different things. Do you like to walk?

I like to play "Tug-of-War" with my daddy.

I like getting petted and hugged.

I like to make new friends.

I like to ride in the car.

See my safety belt?

Sometimes we go camping.

We go to the river.

I like to play at the park.

I like to watch the birds outside.

Mommy made me wear a bow for Christmas.

I don't like it when it rains.

I like to take naps on my comfy bed.

Sometimes I take naps on the floor.

Sometimes I sleep in funny places.

I like to lie in the sun.

It was fun meeting you.
Come play with me some time.

Other children's books by
this author:

Charlie Shepherd The

Witch on Oak Street

Please visit our website at:
www.shalakopress.com

www.ingramcontent.com/pod-product-compliance
Lightning Source LLC
Chambersburg PA
CBHW061149010526
44118CB00026B/2917